Crystal He

CW00449920

A guide to using crystals to balance your chakras

Introduction

You have probably chosen this book as you are interested in crystals and want to learn more about their uses. In this book I will give you a general overview of crystal healing and the use of crystals. We will cover everything you need to know from where to buy crystals, how to cleanse them and how to use them to balance your chakras.

I have included a chapter which introduces the Chakra energy system and gives a brief introduction to each chakra and their positioning on the body. We will then look at each chakra in turn; I have recommended three crystals to help heal and balance each one.

I hope you enjoy this book and find in useful.

Best wishes,

Jayne xx

information is without contract or any type of guarantee assurance.

The trademarks that are used are without any consent, and the publication of the trademark is without permission or backing by the trademark owner. All trademarks and brands within this book are for clarifying purposes only and are the owned by the owners themselves, not affiliated with this document.

Contents

1. Using Crystals

2. Introduction to the Chakras

3. The Root Chakra

4. The Sacral Chakra

5. Solar Plexus

6. The Heart Chakra

7. The Throat Chakra

8. The Third Eye Chakra

9. The Crown Chakra

10. Conclusion

11. Interview with the Author

12. Book Launch Group

13. Free Bonus Chapter

Chapter 1

"Living well and beautifully and justly are all one thing."

Socrates

Using Crystals

Choosing a Crystal

To choose your first crystal, go to a shop that sells crystals and pick out one that you feel drawn to. You may like its colour, size or shape. Maybe you are drawn to pick it up because of its energy. I often find that this is an interesting way of choosing a crystal as you may go home and research that particular crystal and then realise that there is a reason it has come into your life.

The other way to choose a crystal is to research which crystal will help with an area of your life or current health and then go out and buy it. In this book I look at each chakra and give details of the illnesses or health problems that could be caused if a certain chakra is blocked or out of balance.

Please note that if you think you have any medical problems it is best to consult a doctor before trying crystal healing or any other alternative therapies.

Where to buy crystals

Crystals come in many different shapes and sizes from large pieces of nature crystal to small polished tumble stones. It is up to you which size you choose but for the purpose of balancing your chakras I would suggest using a small crystal as it is often good to place the crystal directly on your chakras.

There are a number of places to buy crystals; most cities have new age alternative shops. Look on the internet to see what's available in your area. There are also a number of great online stores.

Another place that I have found to buy crystals is in museum or tourist attraction shops. They often have a stand of crystal and information about each one. This is often cheaper than going to a specialist shop.

Cleansing Crystals

When you first get your crystal it is a good idea to cleanse it before you start using it, this will help to rid it of any energy that it has picked up whilst sitting in a shop and will make sure that it is pure and ready to help heal you.

There are two main ways to cleanse crystals. The first is with water and the second is with the light of the moon or sun. Let's look at these two methods in more detail.

The Moon or Sun

A great way to cleanse your crystals is to put it outside on your windowsill during a full moon. Leave it there all night if possible to recharge its energies, the moons rays will help with the cleansing process.

Alternatively leave your crystal outside during a hot summer's day and the sun's rays will have the same effect.

Water

Water is a great way to cleanse your crystals and is the method that I usually use between full moons. I prefer to use natural fast flowing water. It is great to go for a walk by a river and put your crystals in the water for a few minutes to cleanse them. Being out in nature will also help to recharge you, putting you in a positive mindset.

You could also sit your crystal in a small bowl of water in your home if you don't live near any natural water. Some people would advice putting salt in the water but I wouldn't do this on a regular basis as it can erode the crystals polished surface.

I have however cleansed crystals in the sea.

How to use your Crystals

There are many different ways to use your crystal and different crystal should be placed at different places on the body in order to help balance your chakras. We will look at each chakra in more detail in the following chapters.

Under pillow

Once you have identified which crystal you want to use you could try putting your crystal under your pillow during the night while you sleep. You may like to try this with a crystal that aids sleep or promotes relaxation if you are having problems sleeping.

Alter

Many people also create an alter in their house where they place their crystals, or the crystal that they are currently working with. This may simply be a table where a larger decorative crystal is placed or a more spiritual alter where items of spiritual significance are kept.

Chapter 2

"Life was meant to be lived, and curiosity must be kept alive. One must never, for whatever reason, turn one's back on life."

Eleanor Roosevelt

Introduction to the Chakras

Everything in the universe is made up of energy, including human life. We all have energy flowing through us all the time, whether we are aware of it or not. Before we start discussing the chakras I would like you to feel your energy. Carry out the following exercise.

Energy Exercise

1. Rub your hands together fairly quickly until they become warm.

2. Now open your palms and hold your hands about an inch apart. Can you feel the energy you have created? What does it feel like? Maybe you feel a hot, tingly sensation.

3. Play around with this energy, try rubbing your hands together again and open them a bit further this time. Maybe you would like to move your hands closer then further away to see what effect this has on your energy.

The Chakras

There are seven main centres of energy in the human body and these are known as Chakras. Chakra is a Sanskrit word which means wheel as it is so named because each chakra or energy centre is spinning like a wheel.

The seven chakras are located in a line from the base of your spine to the top of your head. The chakras job is to keep energy flowing in the right direction and in the amount that is needed to each part of the body. A healthy person will have balanced chakras which help guide the mind, body or spirit.

Many common health complains are caused by certain chakras being out of balance, they could be spinning too slowly, too quickly, in the wrong direction or be completely closed. It is possible to function with some chakras out of balance, but for optimal health we need to balance our chakras.

Chakra Meditation

Before teaching you any more about the chakras, I would like to take you through a chakra meditation so that you have a chance to feel the energy in your body and maybe even feel your chakras spinning. Read through these instructions first, then relax and take yourself through the process. Alternatively you could work with a partner and get then to read the instructions to you as you relax.

During this exercise some people will feel their chakras quite intensely, other will feel very little and some people won't feel anything. Your experience of each chakra will probably be different. You might feel some and not others.

1. Find somewhere quite where you won't be disturbed for this exercise. Sit or lie down and take a few deep breaths. Close your eyes so that you can focus inwards. Breathe deeply into the pit of your stomach. You may like to place your hand on your stomach so that you can feel it rising and falling for a few breaths. Begin to feel the energy in your body.

2. Now bring your awareness to the energy that surrounds the base of your spine. This is the location of the first Chakra, known as the root chakra. What do you feel? See if you can feel any energy pulsing or moving. Take a few more deep breaths and continue to feel into your energy.

3. Next move up to your second chakra which is just below your belly button, this is your sacral chakra. As you breathe in notice how this chakra feels. Can you feel any warmth spinning or pulsing?

4. Your third Chakra is called the Solar Plexus and is located a bit above your belly button. This is the chakra that most people feel more intently as it is where you are likely to feel fear or other strong emotions. Tune into this area and see what it feels like.

5. The next chakra is very easy to remember as it is called the heart chakra and it is located where your heart is. Connect with your heart now and see how it feels.

6. The fifth chakra is called your throat chakra and is located in the dip between your collar bones. Can you feel any energy in this area? As you bring your attention to it you may feel the urge to cough or swallow.

7. Bring your attention to your forehead, to the space between your eyes. This is your sixth chakra and is called the Third eye. Can you feel any pulsing or spinning? What is the temperature of this area?

8. Your last chakra is located at the top of your head and is called your crown chakra. What does the energy of this chakra feel like? How does it differ to the other chakras?

9. Take a moment to quietly explore your chakras one at a time. Take a few more deep breaths and then open your eyes.

How to use this book

Now that you have gained a basic understanding of the chakras and where they are located on the body, and perhaps even felt them we will look at each one in more detail. In the following chapters we will look at the location and purpose of each chakra in turn. I will give details of symptoms you may experience if your chakra is blocked and also show you how to tell if they are balanced and in harmony. For each chakra I will recommend three crystals which you can use to balance your chakras.

I would recommend that you read the whole book first and then decide which chakra you would like to work on first. This will probably be a chakra that you are having problems with and that you want to balance. Overtime you can look back at the advice in this book and use it to balance all your chakras; this does however require you buying more crystals.

Alternatively you could look for a chakra balancing set of crystals. Crystals are often sold in sets of seven in new age shops; one for each chakra. You could also consider buying a necklace which contains a small piece of crystal for each chakra.

Chapter 3

"The energy that actually shapes the world springs from emotions."

George Orwell

The Root Chakra

I hope you enjoyed the chakra meditation. Let's get started with looking at the first chakra and how to balance it using crystals. In this chapter I will give you the option of three crystals which could be used to balance the root chakra. You don't need to buy all three, just select the one that you feel more drawn to.

Location & Name

As discussed in the chakra meditation in the last chapter the root chakra is located at the base of the spine. The Root chakras Sanskrit name is muladhara; this is made up of the word Mula which means root and also Dhara which comes from the word support.

Purpose

This chakra has been named as its main function is to help with your survival. The Root chakra helps you stay grounded and strong; it does this by connecting you to the earth. The Root chakra is connected with emotional and financial security. If you are feeling overwhelming emotions or lacking financial abundance then concentrate on balancing your root chakra.

If your root chakra is balanced you will feel safe and secure in yourself. You will feel that the world is a safe place to be and will have security in your life. This could be financial security but also relates to shelter and safety in relationships.

However if your root chakra is out of balance and this is one of the most common chakras to need balancing and realigned, then you may have problems with anxiety and even fear. The root chakra sends messages to the rest of your body that you need to survive, even when there is no real danger. This in turn causes your body to experience symptoms of anxiety. Having an overactive root chakra will often manifest as digestive problems, lower back pain or hip problems. It is also associated with ovarian cysts in woman and prostate problems in men.

Colour

Each chakra has a colour and a symbol connected with it. The Root chakra is red; therefore we will use red crystals to help balance it.

Crystals to balance your Root Chakra

Any crystals that are red in colour are great for balancing the root chakra as this colour is associated with fire and passion but also warmth and vitality. These are all qualities which we need to keep us strong and able to content with whatever life throws at us. There are also a number of crystals of other colours which are great for balancing the root chakra; such as hematite or Smoky Quartz. Carry a red crystal with you at times when you need courage and extra motivation to achieve your dreams. Red Jasper is a great stone for this.

Hematite

Hematite is a great stone for grounding and making you feel more balanced and in harmony as it helps to connect you to the earth and will provide feelings of stability. It is especially useful if you are experiencing inner turmoil which is rife in our modern world.

The Hematite crystal is able to rid you of any negative feelings that may be holding you back from feeling the happiness and vitality that you were born with. If you are feeling stressed or worried about the problems in your life then Hematite is a great crystal to use. It is also great for people who suffer from anxiety. Hematite is one of the best crystals to use for not only your root chakra but also overall healing work as it draws any negative energy stored in the aura towards the root chakra where it is neutralised. This helps to balance all seven chakras.

Traditionally Hematite was used by Viking warriors as it gave them strength and bravery. It was also believed that the stone would help to preserve the life force of injured soldiers who had been wounded during battle; helping them to regain strength and heal.

Smoky Quartz

Are you ready to let more light and positivity into your life? The smoky quartz crystal was traditionally used by Druids as it draws dark of negative energy from the body. It can be used to aid healing in times of despondency and depression. It also helps to release negative emotions such as fear and anger. Smoky quartz is a grounding stone which can help to heal painful memories from the past. Sit quietly with a smoky quartz crystal and meditate on a daily basis to move on from past hurts and avoid becoming bitter.

Smoky quarts can be used to create harmony and balance in the home or work place; as it helps get rid of electromagnetic stress. Our modern life with all its electrical technologies can have a negative effect on our health and wellbeing. Place smoky quarts around the home to help neutralise and return any electric interference to the earth.

This crystal can be placed at the bottom of your feet when you go to sleep at night.

Red Jasper

Red jasper helps with strength, stamina and helps to create a strong connection to the earth. It can help people over come trauma especially trauma related to sexual abuse or domestic violence. Red Jasper helps to ground and balance making you stronger and more able to effectively stand up to dominating people. Wear or meditate with this stone if you are going through any difficulties or life challenges. It is an effective mood stabiliser and can be carried throughout the day in your pocket. In moments when you begin to feel anxious or worried take the stone out and hold in it the palm of your hand for a few minutes.

If you are interested in dreams and researching dream meanings, then sleeping with Red Jasper under your pillow will help you to recall your dreams much more easily.

Grounding Ritual

Choose one of the grounding and root chakra balancing crystals from above. If you are going out to buy a crystal choose the one which resonates the most with you. To start with you may like to energetically cleanse your home or the room you are in with sage as this will help to create a more relaxing environment.

Set an intention for your ritual, for example if you have been feeling depressed then you may like to state that you are letting go of negative thoughts and emotions and that you are handing the situation that has been worrying you over to the universe to resolve.

Lie down or sit in a cross legged position, whichever is most comfortable. Bear in mind that you may fall asleep if you are lying down though. Hold your crystal in your clasped hands and meditate. If you are finding it hard to meditate or are new to meditation then close your eyes and take deep breaths. This will immediately have a calming effect on the mind and body.

Sit quietly for five to fifteen minutes and meditate. Afterwards feel if there is any difference in your energy.

Other ideas

There are many different ways to balance your chakras, using crystals is just one of them. You may like to try a few of the following to get your root chakra healthy and balanced; spending time outside in nature, gardening, swimming or walking.

This chakra can also be calmed with mindfulness techniques such as meditation, yoga or praying and connecting to the universal energy.

Chapter 4

"You only live once. But if you live like me, once is enough."

Frank Sinatra.

The Sacral Chakra

Location and Name

The sacral chakra is located just below the belly button and is connected with how you see yourself as a human being. This chakras Sanskrit name is svadhishana which mean the place of the self. It is connected with creativity and your ability to enjoy life.

Purpose

The main purpose of this chakra is creativity; it works with your life force energy and helps you to enjoy life. The energy of this chakra helps you to indulge in creative pursuits and also motivates you to enjoy sex, good food and other pleasurable activities. By engaging in these activities you will feel a sense of satisfaction and wellbeing.

When your sacral chakra is in balance and functioning as it should you will enjoy life and take pleasure from everything life has to offer without overdoing it.

When this chakra is out of balance you may seek joy and pleasure to the detriment of your health. This could lead to weight problems or addiction. If you are enjoying things a bit too much, things that aren't healthy for you, then your sacral chakra is likely to be out of balance.

If you have been very busy without celebrating your successes and getting enough enjoyment out of life then your chakra is likely to be blocked. Symptoms commonly experienced are depression, decreased sex drive and a lack of passion or motivation for life.

Colour

The sacral chakras colour is orange.

Crystals

Orange, gold or yellow crystals are all great to help balance the sacral chakra. Here's a selection below. As your sacral chakra is located just below your belly button you may like to lie down and place your chosen crystal in your belly button while you meditate.

Carnelian

Carnelian is a great crystal, which can be used for a number of different situations. It helps to balance the sacral chakra as it is helps to improve courage and self-confidence. Wearing Carnelian jewellery will help you get in touch with your creative side. It also helps to encourage feelings of warmth and pleasure. Carnelian will help performers or entertainers as well as public speakers to be more confident and creative, it will help them to come across as warm and friendly.

As the sacral chakra is also concerned with pleasure and sex the carnelian can also help with this area of your life. If you are looking to attract a new romance into your life wear carnelian and rose quartz jewellery over your heart to help you attract a loving partner.

Creative Meditation

Sunset is a great time of day to get creative and meditate with a carnelian crystal as the colours in the sky are echoed in that of the crystal. Looking at the coloured rays of the sun and the range of colours in the sky can be an uplifting experience especially if you are outside in nature.

Hold your Carnelian stone over your sacral crystal and meditate while the sun sets. I often find that it's nice to keep my eyes open for sunset meditation and take deep breaths, letting any thoughts come and go as they arise. Don't get caught up in your thoughts, instead concentrate on your breathing and on watching the sun set.

The final step to the meditation practise is to ask yourself how you can bring more joy and excitement into your life. Meditate on your hearts desires and your dreams. Let your inner child awaken and be in control for a moment. What creative pursuits do you wish to follow? What did you used to enjoy doing as a child? Make an intention to bring more of this activity into your life in order to increase feeling of happiness and joy.

If you have been suffering with low mood lately then you may like to eat a few slices of orange or a piece of pineapple at the end of this ritual. As these fruits are yellow and have nutrients that help nourish your body and increase happiness levels. Eat slowly, savouring every mouthful and continue watching the sunset as you do so.

This ritual along with the Carnelian stone will help you to focus your attention on what really matters in your life; it will help you feel uplifted and more positive.

Tiger's eye

Tiger eye is a brown and tan striped stone which is most commonly mined in South Africa and Thailand. It is a powerful crystal for changing the course of your future when used correctly. It is called tiger eye as it has a unique look which resembles a cat's eye.

This stone is very helpful if you feel like you have problems in different areas of your life, or if you feel overwhelmed with juggling things. This crystal with help you to face up to things with strength and determination and could be said to give you the strength and bravery of a tiger. Any negative feeling of lack will be dispersed and replaced with optimism and clarity.

Citrine

Citrine has a bright yellow and gold colour and is a natural mood up lifter. It helps the user to feel more alive and energised whilst at the same time balancing the sacral chakra. It also helps with creativity and improves your personal power and intelligence.

Other Ideas

The best way to balance this chakra is to make sure you enjoy life, create time for yourself to do the things that you enjoy. You could take up a new hobby or maybe do something you enjoyed when you were younger. Do a painting or drawing.

Make sure that you look after yourself and eat healthy. And of course another way to ensure this chakra is in balance is to make love to your partner.

Chapter 5

"Often intuition will direct your behaviour. If it feels right, it's probably right."

Oprah Winfrey

Solar Plexus

Location and Name

Your third chakra is called the solar Plexus and is located just above the belly button. Its Sanskrit name is Manipura which means lustrous gem. This chakra will help with your self confidence and identity as well as your self esteem.

Purpose

Most people recognise the term, 'having a gut reaction.' This is the place where you feel strong emotions. If you are in a situation that just doesn't feel right then you will feel it in the solar plexus.

When your solar plexus is in balance you will feel your personal power, you will also feel a sense of wisdom. Making decisions will come easily to you and you will seem to know what to do in any situation you are confronted with.

When we give our power away to others then our solar plexus becomes out of balance. By this I mean letting others have too much control over us or our lives. An imbalanced chakra can also be caused by life experiences that are outside of your control. When the solar plexus is out of balance you may feel indecisive, insecure and vulnerable as well as needy. Symptoms that could be suffered are digestive problems or problems with the appendix, pancreas, liver or kidneys.

Colour

The solar plexus colour is yellow

Crystals

Any crystals which are yellow in colour are great for balancing the solar plexus chakra. Here are just a few examples.

Amber

Amber is yellowy orange in colour and is an organic gemstone rather than a crystal. It has been created by nature in a slightly different way to other crystals as Amber is a fossilised tree resin.

Amber is often used to cleanse and balance not just the solar plexus chakra but the aura and whole body. Use amber when you need a boost of confidence or want to increase your mental clarity and stay calm in a crisis. Amber helps to get rid of phobias and fears as well as aiding in stressful situations.

Lemon Quartz

Lemon quartz is another yellow crystal. Like it's bright, sunny colour it has become known as the stone of optimism. It helps to create a happier, more positive disposition and also improves clarity and creativity whist ridding the mind of worry and anxiety. It is also used to balance, activate and clear the energy of the solar plexus chakra.

Lemon quarts will help users to get into a state of deep meditation and will help to improve focus. If you have a large personal goal that you want to complete then it's a good idea to meditate daily with a lemon quartz crystal to help you achieve your dreams.

Yellow Tourmaline

Yellow Tourmaline is a semi-precious stone and therefore will probably cost a little more than other crystals. I have decided to include it in this list however as it is a great stone for not only balancing the solar plexus chakra but also for detoxifying the whole body. It will cleanse the whole system and balance the chakras.

This crystal can also be used to dispel grief and is a great stone to use during rituals as it creates protection.

Solar plexus meditation

To carry out this meditation you will need a yellow crystal, choose from the list above or if you already have a different yellow crystal that will do just as well. Light a white or yellow candle and create a relaxing environment.

Lay on the floor or on your bed and place the yellow crystal over your belly button. Take three slow deep breaths, in through your nose and out through your mouth. You may like to play some meditation music whilst you do this meditation, these can be found on youtube. Continue to lay still, taking regular deep breaths for as long as you like. At least ten minutes is a good amount of time.

Other Ideas

To help balance the solar plexus write a list of all the things that you are good at and everything that you have achieved in your life. This will help improve your self esteem.

As the solar plexus is located at your belly button, you can also try wearing a yellow belt to help keep this chakra in balance and harmony.

Chapter 6

"Some pursue happiness- others create it."

Anonymous

The Heart Chakra

Location and Name

The fourth chakra is called the heart chakra and is located where your heart is. Its sanskrit name is Anahata which means unhurt.

Purpose

This is the chakra that deals with matters of the heart such as love, compassion and kindness. This chakra is also associated with self love and healing. When it is in balance you are able to feel loving and secure. You will feel love and compassion for others as well as for yourself. Even if something happens to temporally upset you or make you angry you will be able to feel compassion for those involved.

If the heart chakra is blocked or out of balance we may make unhealthy decisions in the pursuit of romantic love. Our boundaries may blur. On the other hand you may put the needs of those you love before yourself. You may take care of children and others to the detriment of your own health.

Symptoms of an unbalanced heart chakra include palpitations, heart burn and relationship issues.

Many people have a blocked heart chakra as life tends to give us a lot of heart break. Remember that the universe will only give us what we can handle as a way of teaching us about the world and about ourselves.

Those of us with blocked or unbalanced heart chakras may feel like our heart is blocked off, almost like there is a brick wall around it. We might find it hard to get close to anyone.

Colour

The heart chakras colour is green and pink so any crystal in either of these colours will work well.

Crystals

Rose Quartz

Rose quartz is traditionally known as the stone of the heart, as the name suggests it is pink in colour and is a semi precious stone. It has been used for centauries to help heal and open the heart chakra; making its user feel more loving. This stone can also be used to attract romance into the wearers' life.

Rose quartz is a great crystal to help calm emotional imbalances and promote an overall feeling of peace in the body and mind. It can also help promote a good night's sleep and can help in situations where the user is heart broken or love sick.

Green Calcite

Green calcite is a green, semi precious stone which is used to balance and stimulate the heart chakra and the whole system. It will absorb any negativity from the user and should therefore be cleansed on a regular basis. It is also thought to boost immunity and promote healing and transformation.

This is a great crystal to have around your home or office as it helps to dispel any negative energy and clear any environment that it is placed in. It creates a calming effect whilst removing stagnant energies from your home.

Green Adventurine

Ready for an adventure? Weather that is travel or romance if you have been feeling stuck in a rut recently try meditating with or wearing Adventurine. Adventurine also helps to sooth away any worries, anxieties or negative emotions whilst at the same time helping to increase focus. This crystal will often help people to have a new found confidence in themselves and their abilities.

It is known as the gambling stone and will help promote abundance and luck. The name adventurine comes from an Italian word which means by chance. Warning, the author of this book does not recommend using this stone to gamble but if you do happen to be heading to the casino this weekend maybe put an adventurine crystal in your pocket.

Using heart chakra crystals

Use any of the above crystals to meditate. Lie down and place your crystal on your chest. Alternatively you may like to wear your crystal as a necklace.

Other Ideas

It may be a lot of work to balance your heart chakra, especially if you have experienced a lot of heart ache in your life; whether from romantic relationships or other life situations. Remember that your healing is a process that you have to go through and that this can take time and effort.

The first step in the healing process is to love yourself more. Take some time for yourself on a regular basis and try some of the following ideas.

- Meditate and feel compassion for yourself
- Give yourself a hug
- Have a relaxing bath with candles
- Have a massage

Chapter 7

"You have to leave the city of your comfort
and go into the wilderness of your intuition.
What you'll discover will be wonderful.
What you'll discover will be yourself."
Alan Alda

The Throat Chakra

Location and Name

The fifth chakra is called the throat chakra and is located on
the throat, between your collar bones. Its Sanskrit name is
Vishuddha which mean 'very pure'

Purpose

This chakra relates to communication and gives you the ability
to speak your truth. As your throat chakra is above your heart
it is also connected with the love and compassion you feel for
yourself and others.

When your throat chakra is in balance you will be able to
speak confidently and speak your truth. You will speak to
others with the kindness and compassion that they deserve.
You will be able to advice others when necessary and be able to
say words that are appropriate for the situation.

Our throat chakra becomes overactive when we feel that others
haven't listened to us or we haven't been able to make
ourselves heard. Peoples whose throat chakra is unbalanced
will often interrupt others or speak more loudly than is
necessary. They may have throat problems such as infections
or problems with their mouths such as cavities or ulcers.

Other people with blocked throat chakras feel that they have
been ignored; they shut down their throat chakra and never

speak their truth. They may have problems expressing themselves or feel shy. This often manifests as throat or digestive problems. Energy from the shut down throat chakra is often redirected to the stomach.

Colour

The throat chakras colour is blue.

Crystals

Any crystal which is blue in colour will help to balance the throat chakra, you may like to try one of the following.

Angelite

If you are feeling stressed or angry then Angelite is a great stone to help remove tension from your body and chakra system. It helps to promote forgiveness and understanding if you have been part of an argument or misunderstanding recently. It helps to clear communication channels which can allow for resolution to take place.

This is also a great stone to aid with personal development, whether that is spiritual or the pursuit of psychic insight. Angelite has a deep healing energy which promotes balance and harmony. It helps to sooth the mind and nerves and gives the wearer a feeling of tranquillity. It also helps improve psychic gifts and can be used to help with mental health problems.

Aquamarine

Aquamarines energy is pure and calming, just like the sea. It is the colour of clear, crisp water and has a soothing, cleansing energy. It encourages the letting go of negative situations from the past and promotes relaxation. In ancient times aquamarine was believed to be a stone belonging to the mermaids and sailors often kept a piece in their pockets for good luck and a safe voyage.

Aquamarine is considered a throat chakra stone as it helps to promote clear, deep and meaningful conversation. It helps people to connect more deeply with one another. It also protects those who travel, especially if they are travelling by boat or are near water.

Lapis Lazuli

Lapis Lazuli is a deep, rich blue in colour. It often contains speaks of gold or white, which are calcite and pyrite deposits. These stones are considered good luck and promote abundance and prosperity.

This stone helps to promote spiritual renewal. Whilst meditating with this crystal you may like to bring to mind images of the sea, sky and other natural waters such as lakes and rivers.

Meditation

Lay down somewhere where you won't be disturbed and meditate with a blue crystal on your throat chakra; in the dip between your collar bones. This will help to balance your throat chakra. You can also wear a blue crystal as a necklace to help keep it balanced throughout the day.

Other Ideas

In order to balance your throat chakra you need to start speaking your truth and expressing your emotions. It is also important to think before you speak.

Chapter 8

"Most people are about as happy as they make up their minds to be."

Abraham Lincoln

The Third Eye Chakra

Location and Name

The sixth chakra is called the Third Eye, it is located on your forehead between your eyes. In Sanskrit this chakra is called Ajna which means 'beyond wisdom' as this is the chakra which deals with your psychic abilities.

Purpose

This chakra connects you to the spiritual world and gives you your intuition or even psychic abilities. People who are on a spiritual path aim to achieve balance in the third eye chakra. When this chakra is in balance you will feel like everything in life is flowing. You will be in tune with both the material world and the spiritual realms.

If your third eye is out of balance you will become either too materialistic or too interested in paranormal experiences to the point where activities like reading tarot cards have an unhealthy impact on your life.

Most people have a blocked third eye chakra to some extent as we live in a more materialistic world which doesn't value intuitive or psychic development. We often feel disconnected from our spirituality. If this is the case you may suffer from headaches or have allergies and sinus problems.

Colour

The third Eye's colour is indigo

Crystals

Any purple, lilac or indigo crystal is great for healing and balancing the third eye chakra.

Amethyst

Amethyst is a semi precious stone which is available in a variety of shades of purple. Its main use is to open, heal and balance the third eye chakra whilst offering wisdom. It also helps to protect wearers from harm and negative energies.

Amethyst is a great stone to use in meditation as it is a calming stone which works over different planes to promote peace and harmony. Amethyst works in the emotional, spiritual and physical planes so can be used to heal a number of ailments and also helps to improve psychic gifts.

Indigo Kyanite

Indigo Kyanite is traditionally used in the eastern world to restore QI (pronounced chee) to the body. It is also used to promote a calming effect which will balance and harmonise the whole system. This stone can be bought in a range of blue and purple colours and its energy is particularly helpful for healing and balancing both the third eye and the throat chakra. Therefore it can help with both communications; associated with the throat chakra and psychic awareness associated with the third eye chakra.

Purple Fluorite

Purple Fluorite is another stone which is used to stimulate and balance the third eye chakra as well as the whole chakra system in general. It is a semi precious stone which helps to get rid of any negativity whilst also improving mental clarity. If you are suffering from brain fog then this is a great crystal as it helps to improve focus.

Purple fluorite is also a great stone to use if you want to improve psychic ability and intuition.

Meditation for the third eye

In order to open the third eye chakra we need to be in balance and harmony with nature. We need to be grounded in reality as an unbalance third eye chakra can lead to living in a fantasy world.

In order to achieve this you may like to do a grounding meditation. Stand outside in a garden or park with bare feet. Make sure you feet are hip width apart and that you are standing strong with the soles of your feet rooted into the ground. If you choose to, you can hold a purple crystal in one or both hands.

Take three deep breaths, slowly in through your nose and out through your mouth. Then sigh deeply letting any stress evaporate from your body. Stand tall and take three more, slow deep breaths. Close your eyes and relax into the meditation. Take a further three deep breaths. See how you feel.

If you would like to continue to meditate you can sit down in a cross legged position or lay on the ground with your crystal. If you decide to lie down you can place your crystal on your forehead.

Other Ideas

Spend some time in meditation to help balance your third eye chakra; see if you can connect to your third eye chakra. It may also be helpful to get out in nature more often, go to the beach and dig your toes into the sand to help ground yourself.

Chapter 9

"The purpose of life is to live it."

Clarence Darrow

The Crown Chakra

Location and Name

The 7th chakra is located at the top of the head and is called the crown chakra. Its Sanskrit name is Sahaswara which means 'thousand petaled' this chakra is conscious energy. The energy from the universe will flow through you into your crown chakra and this is a very pure energy.

Purpose

This chakra helps to connect us to the entire universe. The universe gives us energy to sustain our life here on earth. It is not easy to achieve balance in the crown chakra and those that have are said to have had a spiritual awakening or achieved a state of nirvana in Buddhism. It is the journey to balancing our crown chakra that brings us happiness, wisdom and good health. If you try to balance your crown chakra it will help to balance your other six chakras.

Having a crown chakra that is out of balance just means that you are having a human experience, therefore it is better to attempt to balance your other chakras to achieve greater balance in your crown chakra.

Colour

The colour of the crown chakra is violet-white. It is more like an infra red colour on the colour spectrum and is a special colour and pure energy.

Crystals

Any crystal which is clear, white or purple is great for healing the crown chakra.

Selenite

Selenite is a clear, mineralised crystal which helps to activate and open the third eye and crown chakra. I often like to buy crystals which have multiple uses and help with different chakras and this is one such stone. Selenite helps to clear and activate the whole system and also cleanses the aura.

It clears away any congested energy from the brain and mind; in this way the stone can help with any mental problems as well as helping to lift awareness to higher realms. It helps to remove any blocks which may have been holding you back in life and allows you to follow your dreams and achieve goals more easily.

Clear Quartz

Clear quartz is another crystal which has a number of uses, one of the main ones being that it amplifies energy. It also helps improve spiritual awareness and opens and expands the crown chakra. It can be used to aid conversation with spirit guides and encourages psychic clarity.

Health wise; clear quarts helps to stimulate the nervous system and also promotes the growth of hair and fingernails.

Charoite

I have included charoite here as this crystal has a lovely gentle energy; it is a great crystal for beginners as it can help you to connect to spiritual work.

Charoite is a good crystal to use while you are sleeping; put your crystal under your pillow before you go to bed. It will help you to release old, negative energy patterns which no longer serve you, whilst at the same time improving the frequency of your energies vibrations.

Meditation to help balance the crown chakra

As your crown chakra is connected to both the spiritual world and the physical world it is important to meditate regularly in order to keep it balanced. A balanced crown chakra will help you to achieve your ambitions and attract the things that you want into your life. I hope the following meditation helps.

Sit somewhere quiet where you won't be disturbed, hold a white or purple crystal in your hands and take three deep breaths. Now imagine a halo of golden light around your head. Continue to breathe deeply and meditate, keeping this golden light in mind.

Imagine the light is healing and balancing your crown chakra, let go of anything that comes up that no longer serves you or that you no longer need in your life. Meditate in this way for 10 to 15 minutes. If your attention wanders, bring your mind back to imagining the golden light. Create a feeling of warmth inside your body as you do so. Know that you are both loved and supported in all that you do. You are loved from beings in the spiritual as well as the physical world.

When you have finished your meditation; take three, final, long deep breaths in before slowly opening your eyes. How do you feel? How does your head feel? Do you have any sensations in your body? Pay special attention to the area around your crown chakra, how does that feel.

Other Ideas

Meditate and connect to your spirit guide on a daily basis, feel the universal energy flowing through your crown chakra.

Conclusion

I hope that you enjoyed learning about crystals and how to use them to balance your chakras. Continue to work with your crystals on a daily basis to get the best results.

Thanks again for downloading Crystal Healing: A guide to using crystals to balance your chakras.

If you enjoyed this book please leave me a review on Amazon. You may also like to check out some of the other books I've written. I have included a free bonus chapter from my book Design Your Life: A guide to manifesting the life you deserve.

Good luck!!

Other Publications Include

Design Your Life: A Guide to manifesting the life you deserve!

https://www.amazon.com/Design-Your-Life-manifesting-productivity-ebook/dp/B07G7Z616T

Money Matters: Manifest Money by changing your financial Vibes in order to Thrive!

https://www.amazon.com/Money-Matters-financial-manifesting-attraction-ebook/dp/B07GDM7Z6T

Crystal Healing: A Guide to Using Crystals to Balance your Chakras!

https://www.amazon.com/Crystal-Healing-balancing-alternative-beginners-ebook/dp/B07KPLCY3J

Anxiety Help: Overcome Anxiety, Panic, Stress and Worry fast!

https://www.amazon.com/Anxiety-Help-Overcome-techniques-Supplements-ebook/dp/B07G676GYW

Brave Honest Healing: The Best of the Blog

https://www.amazon.com/Brave-Honest-Healing-alternative-mindfulness-ebook/dp/B07LFKC5JY

Brave Honest Healing: e- magazine- Winter edition

https://www.amazon.com/Brave-Honest-Healing-magazine-resolutions-ebook/dp/B07MGPFKTJ

Happy Now:30 Day Happiness Challenge

https://www.amazon.com/Happy-Now-meditation-alternative-Spirituality-ebook/dp/B07MBT4KY4

Interview with the Author

Tell us about yourself and how many books you have written.

I'm a writer, blogger and personal development enthusiast. I created Brave. Honest.Healing to help other improve their well being and create the life they have always dreamed of. I have written a number of books that help add value to readers lives and help solve any problems they are currently facing. I have written and self published seven books on kindle.

What is the name of your latest book and what inspired it?

My latest book is called Crystal Healing: A guide to using Crystals to Balance your Chakras. I published it last month and am very happy with how it has turned out. I have always loved nature and been interested in Crystals in particular. When I was 21 I was attuned to practise Reiki and I began using crystals to help balance my chakras. In this book I have put together all the knowledge I have acquired over the last seven years on how to balance the chakras using crystals.

Do you have any unusual writing habits?

I like to write in the mornings and I use a website called focus mate to keep me motivated and give me the accountability to keep going!

What authors, or books have influenced you?

I love anything by Joanne Harris especially Chocolate. Another book that has influenced me is the 4 hour work week by Tim Ferriss as it has made me question societies traditional beliefs about how to make a living and inspired me to start my own business.

What are you working on now?

I recently walked the Camino de Santiago – a 560 mile walk across Spain. I am writing a book about the inspiration I gained on the walk and the people I met. I'm hoping it will be published early next year.

What is your best method or website when it comes to promoting your books?

I have put my book on promotion on kindle which has been effective. I am still new to learning how to market my book and hope that I will get better at it in the future.

Do you have any advice for new authors?

Write every day, it is easier to get in the habit of writing if you make an effort to write small chunks every day. If you are working on a book and it feels daunting it is easier to come up with an outline and then write a paragraph at a time. You will soon have your book written.

What is the best advice you have ever heard?

I think the best advice I have heard is to read a lot as this will help improve your writing.

What are you reading now?

The Miracle Morning – it is helping me to get into better habits in the morning so that I start off the day on a positive note.

What's next for you as a writer?

I have a lot of ideas for new books and need to make the time to get them written. I would like to write a fiction book and have a great idea for a story about a family that are working with a travelling fair. It is a magical story and the family are making potions to help people solve their problems whilst at the same time running away from problems of their own. At the end they are forced to confront their problems head on and their lives are changed for the better.

If you were going to be stranded on a desert island and allowed to take 3 or 4 books with you what books

would you bring?

Chocolate by Joanne Harris

A year of Marvellous Ways by Sarah Winman

The Travelling Cat Chronicles by Hiro Arikawa

Book Launch Group

Hi I am starting a book launch group and am looking for new people to join. If you are interested in reading, personal development and reviewing then this opportunity could be for you.

My name is Jayne Todd and I have an e-book publishing company called Brave.Honest.Healing I write personal development and self help books on a number of topics including health and fitness, diet and lifestyle, meditation and alternative spirituality. Most recently I have published a book about dealing with anxiety, a book about crystal healing and two books about manifesting. I am currently writing a book about meditation and have many more ideas for future projects.

In order for you to take part you would need to have an Amazon account or be willing to create one. I would like to offer you free books as they are published in return for your feedback and would also like you to write an honest review on Amazon. You don't need to read every book I publish but can pick and choose the subjects that you are interested in.

If this sounds like something you'd want to get involved in send me an email (bravehonesthealing@yahoo.com) with a bit about yourself and we can get started.

Thanks for your help

Jayne

Chapter 1 – Bonus Chapter

Design Your Life: A Guide to manifesting the life you deserve!

What is a Vision Board

A vision board is a tool which can be used to manifest your desires. It can help you to focus on certain areas of your life or to look at your life as a whole. Vision boards are created from images that you have collected from various sources such as magazines or the internet.

A lot has been written about manifesting and there seems to be two schools of thought. The first is that by putting your attention onto an area of your life and creating a vision board for it you will have started to create a shift. Some people have reported creating a vision board and putting it away in a draw and forgetting about it. They then carry on with their life and when they look at it again in six months time they realise that they have unconsciously created everything that they put on their board, or at least most of the things. Is this just a coincidence?

I believe that after creating a vision board it is better to take inspired action towards achieving the life you want. I have my vision board displayed in my bedroom and stop and look at it every day. However for years this is as far as I went. I had a board on my wall and looked at it every now and again, some of the things seemed to occur in my life and other seemed like they were just a distant dream. I was trying to manifest but was stuck in the wanting stage and hadn't yet moved into the receiving stage. I became frustrated and didn't believe that I was able to change my life.

I then came up with a strategy to really motivate and focus my attention on achieving the life I wanted. I had just turned thirty and was fed up with the life that society thinks we should be leading. I felt that I hadn't achieved the career success or relationship goals that other people seemed to. I began to compare myself negatively with other people. Then I realised that if anything was going to change I needed to make the changes myself.

Here's how I made my vision board work for me.

1. I created a brand new vision board. First I did a meditation to calm my mind and get me into a positive state. I allowed myself to dream and to visualise the life I really wanted.

2. Then I got my stake of magazines and began to flick through them whilst listening to relaxing music. I used meditation music but you may like to try more uplifting or energising music. What ever gets you in a creative inspiring mood. I cut out the images that inspired me, the images of things that I wanted to create in my life. I cut out images of fruit to represent better health and of a beach as this was the dream location for my new house.

3. Once I had finished my vision board I put it on the wall where I would see it regularly. I then looked at each image individually and really started to think about why I wanted it and how I was going to get it to show up in my life. I wrote down a goal for how I was going to achieve each of the things on my board.

For example as fruit represents health I decide that I would make a fruit smoothie every day to improve my health. I immediately got my blender out of the cupboard, where it had been gathering dust. Washed it and left it in the kitchen where I would see it on a daily basis to remind me to make a smoothie.

I came up with similar strategies for each image.

4. Each morning I looked at my vision board and meditated in front of it. I visualised having the things I wanted in my life. Each day I also read my list of goals and I asked myself. What

can I do today to bring me closer towards achieving this version of my life? After a month I realised that I had made a lot of positive changes in my life. It only takes 30 days for new habits to be formed and I was able to introduce positive life style changes and make them stick. As these changes became a habit I did them automatically and was then able to make other changes. In this way I was able to achieve my whole list of goals in a fairly short space of time. Even though when I initially read my list of goals it seemed overwhelming and like it was a lot to take on. I felt that I wouldn't have the time to achieve them all but in the end was able to initiate them into my life. After a while I realised that I had almost all the things on my vision board in my life. It was time to create a new, even more ambitious vision board.

Task

Create your own vision board either for your whole life's vision or for an area of your life that you feel you need to improve e.g. Relationship, finances or career. Follow my steps above to create lasting positive changes in your life.

In the next chapter we will move on to creating a written vision board which I have found to be even more effective and powerful in creating the life you want. It is important to take the first step and create a traditional vision board with images.

Printed in Great Britain
by Amazon

29046028R00030